First Weeks

Baby Tips™
The Little Terror

Other books in the Baby Tips™ series
by Charlotte Preston and Trevor Dunton

The Little Terror: Good Sleeping Guide
The Little Terror: Good Feeding Guide
The Little Terror: Good Behavior Guide

First Six Weeks

Baby Tips™
The Little Terror

CHARLOTTE PRESTON, RN   TREVOR DUNTON

~: for Alfie, Sophie, Tilly, Theo, Emilio and Sofia :~

Publishers: Howard W. Fisher, Helen V. Fisher

Managing Editor: Sarah Trotta

Book Production: Randy Schultz

Illustrations: Trevor Dunton

Cover Design: Randy Schultz

Published by Fisher Books, LLC
5225 W. Massingale Road
Tucson, Arizona 85743
(520) 744-6110

Printed in U.S.A.
Printing 5 4 3 2 1

Library of Congress Cataloging-in-Publication Data
Preston, Charlotte, 1935-
  [Little terror's first six weeks]
  The Little Terror. First six weeks / Charlotte Preston,
Trevor Dunton. — North American ed.
     p. cm. — (Baby Tips for new moms and dads)
  Originally published: The little terror's first six weeks.
London : Metro Books, 1998.
  ISBN 1-55561-199-0
  1. Infants—Care. 2. Infants (Newborn) 3. Parenting.
4. Parent and infant. I. Dunton, Trevor. II. Title.
III. Title: First six weeks. IV. Title: First 6 weeks. V. Series.
HQ774.P74 1999
649'.122dc21   99-36914
                                                                      CIP

First published in Great Britain in 1998 by Metro Books, an imprint of Metro Publishing Limited,
19 Gerrard Street, London W1V 7LA

North American edition © 1999 Fisher Books, LLC
Text © 1998, 1999 Charlotte Preston and Trevor Dunton
Illustrations © 1999 Trevor Dunton

Notice: The information in this book is true and complete to the best of our knowledge. It is offered with no
guarantees on the part of the authors or Fisher Books. Authors and publisher disclaim all liability with use of
this book.

An extra note for parents with girls:
You'll find that throughout the Little Terror books we refer to babies as "he."
Please don't think we've neglected your daughters! It's purely in the interests of clarity and space.
Using he/she, his/her, himself/herself is cumbersome to read and uses valuable space that we wanted to
devote to more useful topics. So, please read "she" for "he."

Contents

DON'T PANIC!

This book is about helping you survive your Little Terror's first six weeks. Like many soon-to-be parents, you probably spent the last nine months in a countdown mode, preparing for the big day. You may have attended all the classes conscientiously and read all the books until you were expert on the three stages of labor, could recognize a contraction and had breathing pretty much mastered. However, birth is such a momentous, daunting and wonderful event all by itself that it's easy to forget what happens on the other side.

Suddenly, there you are on your doorstep, proudly holding your own very real Little Terror (LT) in your arms and wondering how on earth you will cope.
DON'T PANIC!

Before you know it, you'll be the world's leading expert on that warm bundle you're holding. This book is designed to give you a head start and, if nothing else, to reassure you that you're doing just fine.

We have broken down the first six weeks into the following topics:

- Coming home
- Feeding—breast or formula?
- The crying game—burping and sleeping
- Washing and bathing
- Diapers
- Taking LT out
- Health and safety

Don't Panic!

COMING HOME

First steps in a new life

Bringing your new baby home is special.
Probably about now it begins to dawn on
you that life will never be the same again.

Wonderful—yes; exhausting—definitely. You won't have time for anything besides caring for your baby and, we hope, yourselves. You'll feel very tired, both from lack of sleep and recovering from the delivery. You'll find day merging into night in a continuous spiral of feeding, burping and diaper-changing. You have to learn so many things at once that it may seem overwhelming. You may be afraid you won't be able to cope.

Don't worry, in a few weeks it really does get better. Before you know it, you'll be looking back fondly at this time when everything was new, and you and LT were just getting to know each other.

Try to enjoy it!

Unlike sleep, one thing you definitely won't lack is advice. Everyone, from the local bank clerk to Mrs. Knowitall next door, thinks they're a childcare expert. Follow your own instincts. Remember, this is your baby. Do what is right for you.

MRS KNOWITALL

Blah Blah Blah...

First Six Weeks

Mood swings and depression

The first few weeks can be an emotional roller coaster for any new mom. If you feel blissfully happy one minute and then hopeless and tearful the next, you could have the "baby blues." It's easy to underestimate how exhausted you are. Plus, your hormones are going through an adjustment period. If you feel unsteady, be kind to yourself. You'll start getting back to normal in about six weeks.

If the feeling doesn't improve, or gets worse, you may have postnatal depression. If you don't seem to be getting better, and possibly are having problems bonding with your baby, share your worries with someone right away.

Let your partner or a close friend know how awful you feel. Their support might be enough to get you through. Tell your doctor, who may prescribe medication and can refer you to a counselor. With the right help, you'll be fine.

About Dad

Becoming a father is a strange and wondrous experience. You'll be pulled in every direction by all kinds of unfamiliar emotions.

You may have been through the birth at your partner's side, seen your baby born and held him or her in your arms. Then suddenly you're back at home, wondering what hit you. When she comes home, your partner, who used to be fairly reasonable, is having Jekyll-and-Hyde-type mood swings. You can't seem to do anything right, and every conversation is about diapers, burping or colic! What are you supposed to be doing, anyway?

If you feel left out, even jealous, remember you can make a big difference in LT's first six weeks. First, by supporting and helping your partner as much as you can, and then, by getting involved yourself! LT is your baby too, and you need to get to know each other. It won't be

Polish up your diaper-changing techniques

long before one of those special Little Terror smiles gets you *right there*, and it might just surprise you to find that you can quiet your wailing LT even better than Mom.

Not to mention the serious satisfaction a slick job of diaper-changing can bring.

Bonding

Bonding is nature's way of making sure you put up with your Little Terror when he is causing you some serious grief, and that you continue to do so throughout his childhood and beyond. Many mothers feel very attached to their babies before or immediately after birth, but don't worry if you don't. It can take a couple of weeks, or even longer.

Sex and contraception

Discuss how you feel with your partner. It's likely you'll be more interested in sleep at this stage. If you're still very sore, sex is probably the last thing on your mind, but it is safe to make love as soon as you both feel ready (this might be before your six-week checkup or after several months).

Note: You will need contraception. Don't assume you're safe while you are still breastfeeding, or before your periods resume, unless you want Little Terror II on your hands.

SURVIVAL TIPS

Get help! Drag in trusted friends and relatives, even if they just baby-sit for half an hour or cook a meal while you nap or take a bath. You owe yourself a break and you will feel even more loving toward

your baby afterward. If you are fine, he will be fine too.

🍼 **Doctors and nurses are there to help.** If you're worried, don't hesitate to contact them. You'll probably be in touch with doctors more in LT's first year than for the rest of his life.

🍼 **Talk to your partner.** Parenting is tough for both of you. Give each other support.

FEEDING—
BREAST OR FORMULA?

To help you decide whether to breast- or bottle-feed, here are some pros and cons of both. Remember, it is your choice. Whichever method you decide to use, if it's right for you, it's right!

Breastfeeding—The good things:

🍼 It's custom-made for LT, containing everything he needs for health and development.

🍼 It's natural and easy to digest. Breastfed babies have fewer stomach aches and constipation than bottle-fed babies.

🍼 Breast milk contains antibodies that protect LT from infections. He's less likely to get sick.

✂ He'll benefit even if you breastfeed for just the first couple of weeks.

✂ Breast milk also seems to protect your baby from developing eczema later.

✂ It costs nothing, no preparation is needed, and it is available 24 hours a day, sterile and at the right temperature.

✂ If LT is premature, breast milk will give him a very special start.

🐞 LT can be bottle-fed by others using your expressed breast milk.

🐞 Breastfeeding is the natural way to use up the energy stores (fat) that build up during pregnancy. Or, to put it another way, breastfeeding is nature's weight-loss program!

The not-so-good things:

🍼 Only LT's mom can produce the goods.

🍼 Dad can only be involved in feeding if Mom has expressed her milk.

☙ You may worry because you can't see how much LT has eaten.

☙ Feeding can seem to take forever at first because it takes time to get the hang of it.

☙ Breastfeeding can be tiring.

Bottle-feeding with formula—
The good things:

🎀 Dad can try it.

🎀 It is easier to leave LT with
his dad, grandma or a
friend when you go out.

🎀 The feedings take less time.

🎀 It's an alternative if you don't like the thought of breastfeeding.

The not-so-good things:

🍼 You will need time and energy to prepare each bottle.

🍼 Formula costs money!

🍼 LT will be less protected from tummy aches, infections and allergies.

Breastfeeding

With a little luck, breastfeeding will work for both you and LT from the start. But it can take more than three weeks to get established. In the early stages, your hospital nurse can help you sort out problems and get LT latched on correctly so feeding doesn't hurt. After that, you can contact your local La Leche League leader for breastfeeding help. Look in the telephone book or ask your doctor.

Before . . .

Successful breastfeeding depends on LT's mom being relaxed, confident and not too exhausted. For the first day or two, your breasts will provide a thick yellow liquid called *colostrum*. This has all the nutrients he needs and will protect him from infection. Offer him this as soon after his birth as you can to stimulate the hormones used to make milk.

. . . After

Breastfeeding works by supply and demand—the more LT drinks, the more milk you produce. LT's sucking causes the let-down reflex in your breast so that the milk flows to your nipple. At first, just hearing LT cry can cause the let-down reflex, and your breasts might leak a little (use breast pads in your bra, and change them frequently).

Tips for soothing uncomfortable breasts

Before a feeding, the breasts fill with milk and can become hard and uncomfortable. This feeling is relieved when the milk starts to flow. If your breasts become uncomfortable:

⚘ Take immediate action and try expressing a little milk before each feed. This can also help avoid mastitis (inflamed or blocked milk ducts).

🎀 Take a hot shower or bath. This can help the flow.

🎀 If your breasts are hot and painful, try putting cold compresses of frozen peas (seriously!) or (even stranger) cabbage leaves inside your bra. Some people swear by them!

40

🔔 Acetaminophen (such as Tylenol®) can help you through the first few days.

🔔 Don't stop breastfeeding or offer a bottle.

Tips for problem-free breastfeeding

🍼 Feed LT frequently, letting him stay on one breast as long as he wants. Then offer him the other. Remember to switch breasts at the next feeding. The watery milk you express first is for quenching his thirst. The rich milk that follows helps him grow. Don't give bottles at night, because nighttime breastfeeding helps build up your milk supply.

🐚 Even if things aren't going too well, keep trying. You are giving LT something very special and once you stop, you can't start again.

🐚 Let him feed on demand. Don't watch the clock or take him off the breast before he's finished. If he wets 6 diapers a day and is gaining weight, he is getting enough milk. Don't expect a feeding routine for the first four to six weeks.

🎀 As LT's mom, you need to take care of yourself so you can provide all that nutritious breast milk. Dad can help by bringing you a cup of herbal tea and a snack (new mothers often say they don't have time to eat). You will need a lot of support and encouragement while learning to breastfeed.

Getting comfortable

The right position is important for successful breastfeeding. Sit and hold him close with his head and body facing you, or lie on your side with LT lying alongside with his nose in line with your nipple. Wait until his mouth is wide open and bring him to your breast (not vice versa) so that he can take in your nipple and the area around it, including part of the breast below the nipple. Don't hold him away from you so that he pulls on your breast— let him rest his head in the crook of your arm.

When he is latched on, make sure his chin is against your breast and his lower lip is turned out. Let LT take the nipple. Don't push it into his mouth, because his tongue will move against the nipple instead of the breast, causing sore nipples. Once in position, LT will suck deeply for most of the feeding and stop sucking when he has had enough. It's normal for him to stop and start a little, pulling his head away from time to time.

Let him feed on the first breast until he is full. Then burp him if you want to and offer the second breast.

Dad can help by
bringing you a snack

First Six Weeks

If he has had enough after one breast, remember to offer the other breast first at the next feeding. It won't take long to work out what is best for you and LT.

Bottle-feeding with formula

Formula milk is cow's milk that has been modified to be as much like mother's milk as possible. Just to confuse you, there are lots of different brands. Make sure you start with one labeled "first" because some are for older babies and will be harder for LT to digest.

Feeding is a time to get close to LT. It's important to be comfortable, relaxed and unhurried. Get as much support as you can. You will need both help and rest to make feedings enjoyable for you and your baby.

Washing and sterilizing

To wash the bottles and nipples, use dish soap in water, squirting it through the nipples and using a bottle brush for the bottles. Get rid of any trace of milk, because old milk harbors germs, and LT is especially vulnerable during the first few weeks.

There are several different ways to sterilize bottles and nipples. Steam sterilizers are quick and efficient. You can also buy special microwave bottle sterilizers. The dishwasher is another option, although the water temperature must be at least 180 F (82 C) and this

Old milk harbors germs

method will wear out the nipples.

Before chemicals and gadgets, moms used to boil the bottles in a saucepan for 5 minutes to kill germs. You can still use this method for emergencies.

Be prepared

Before you bring LT home, you will need 6 bottles and nipples. With many different types and sizes available, you'll need to experiment to find the nipple that flows at the right rate for LT. Have supplies of formula milk and sterilizing equipment on hand to last for the first few days.

Tips for successful bottle-feeding

Always wash your hands before preparing a bottle. To start with, LT will probably eat little and often. Feed him on demand. As long as his weight is OK, let him decide how much he wants. There's no need to force food. Crying does not always mean that he's hungry (see the following section on crying).

Formula labels are a general guide to how often and how much to feed your baby, but this will vary because all babies are different. Never add extra scoops, which can cause dehydration, or use less formula, because he won't get enough nourishment.

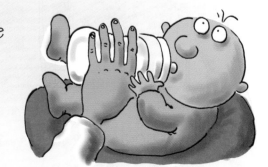

Most babies, whether breast- or bottle-fed, lose weight in the first few days, but they usually return to their birth weight by 2 to 3 weeks old.

If you bottle-feed regularly, give your baby cooled, boiled water between feedings, because he may get thirsty.

First Six Weeks

Preparing a bottle

Boil the water and pour the right amount
into the bottle. Let it cool, then measure the
formula with the scoop and add it to the
bottle. Shake well. You can make up several
bottles at a time and keep prepared bottles
in the refrigerator for up to 24 hours. Throw
away unused milk after this time period.
Don't use bottled water.

Nipples that are too small can cause LT to suck too hard. He will get tired and take in too much air. On the other hand, if nipples are too large, LT will gulp and spit up, get frustrated and, again, take in too much air. Change the nipple if it becomes blocked. If a nipple flattens during a feeding, pull on the bottle gently to release the vacuum.

Be sure the milk isn't coming out too fast . . .

Mixing breast- and bottle-feeding

This is an option after breastfeeding is well established.

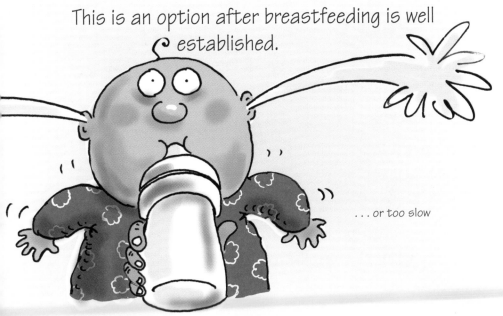

. . . or too slow

There are several reasons for choosing this path:

- You may be a reluctant breastfeeder and about to give up entirely. If this is the case, it's still better for LT to have had some breast milk than none at all.
- You might be very tired and desperate for a rest.
- You might be returning to work and want to introduce a bottle gradually.

THE CRYING GAME—
BURPING AND SLEEPING

If Little Terror's first cry is music to your ears, it isn't necessarily a tune that improves the more times you hear it. If, during serious bouts of wailing, you find your inner smile wearing thin, remember that all over the world thousands of other parents are going through the same thing.

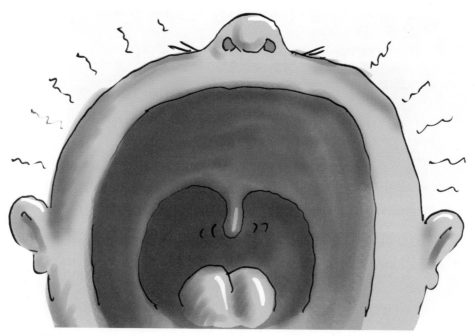

First Six Weeks

Crying is normal. All babies do it, some more, some less, for a variety of reasons. Your Little Terror might be more sensitive to his surroundings than other babies and more easily disturbed.

Remember that you can only do your best. Get as much practical help as you can from close friends or relatives, even if they just take LT for a trip to the mall. Take care of yourselves and try to catch up on lost sleep. Good luck.

See also the end of this section for a checklist of the causes of crying and how to handle them.

All *about* crying

Before he starts talking, crying is the only
way Little Terror can communicate. He'll let
you know when he's hungry, thirsty, sleepy
or has gas, when he doesn't want a bath or

would prefer you leave his diaper off, thanks. He might be just a little fed up, or unhappy about being put down to sleep. You'll discover lots of reasons why your Little Terror cries, and all of them are normal.

You will soon learn to distinguish between a sudden scream: *I could be in pain, please respond right away!*—and a whimpering cry: *It might be worth leaving me for a few minutes to see if I'll calm down on my own.*

For the first three months, babies are not able to cry at will. However, after this time, if LT keeps on crying for long periods, he may have learned that you will always respond.

No one really knows why, but babies all over the world cry most in the evening. If your baby cries a lot, it's easy to feel inadequate. Remember there is no evidence that normal crying harms babies. It bears no relation to anything you did or didn't do. It's a lottery. It's not your fault.

How much crying is normal?

You may have a Little Treasure from the start, who cries very little, or a Little Terror who cries for 3 hours a day.

Both are normal. Average crying time is about 2 hours in 24. Even if it seems to you that he is crying all the time, your LT is probably no worse than any other, but you suffer for every second. If he really won't stop, and you are worried, seek medical advice.

Crying time usually peaks at 6 weeks and then drops to half of that by about

3 months. This is because colic (which is related to digestive problems and causes tummy pain) and burping get better at about this time.

Why is he crying?

Use the following checklist for quick reference to help you decide why your baby is crying and what to do about it.

CHECK LIST

1. **Hungry?** Feed on demand.
2. **Diaper full?** Change it.
3. **Has gas?** Help him burp. See page 80.
4. **Too hot or cold?** What are you wearing? He needs a little more on than you.

Diaper full?

5 Tired? Calm him down with a walk. Put him in a carrying sling, stroller or baby swing.

6 Wants cuddling? Cuddle him freely.

7 Wants to suck? It's OK to use a pacifier.

8 Upset with his milk? Check your diet if breastfeeding; if bottle-feeding, check the type and strength of formula.

⑨ **Constipated?** Extra water (if bottle-feeding), then very diluted orange or prune juice.

⑩ **Not feeling well?** Check that nothing is seriously wrong. If he is sick, seek medical advice immediately.

⑪ **Life too hectic?** Slow down.

⑫ **Screaming in the tub?** Afterward, try calming him with a baby massage.

Too much air

When LT gulps milk and swallows a lot of air with it, he feels discomfort. The air gets trapped and causes pain. The cure for this is burping. Hold LT upright against your shoulder or support him sitting up, and pat or rub his back to help him burp. He might bring up some milk as you are burping him. A towel over your shoulder may come in handy for cleanup!

If LT has colic, it's painful and he'll scream like crazy, lift up his legs and hopefully pass some serious gas! Colic is caused by his immature intestine

First Six Weeks

going into a spasm and making bubbles of air, which have to come out of one end or the other. The bad news is, it's very upsetting. The good news is, it gets better by about 3 months.

Sleep

When Mrs. Knowitall tells you *her* baby slept for 29 hours a day, don't believe it! New babies are generally awake for about 8 hours a day, and they sleep for varying amounts of time at a stretch.

Unreasonably, LT won't fit in with your sleep routine, so you need to sneak in a nap whenever you can.

Introduce good sleeping habits right from the start by trying to get LT to go to sleep on his own once a day. Instead of nursing or cuddling him to sleep, rock him in his swing or push him in his stroller. Pat him or sing to him. Many new parents don't realize that it's OK to put LT down awake. **Note:** on his back.

WASHING AND BATHING

It's normal for first-time parents to feel overwhelmed and scared at the thought of these enormous tasks. After all, your baby looks so fragile! But don't panic. After the first couple of weeks, you'll probably wonder what you were so worried about.

It's normal to feel like this

Washing

You don't have to give LT a full bath every day. You can just wash his face, neck, hands and then his bottom. To do this you will need warm water in a plastic bowl (use your elbow to check that it's not too hot), a towel, cotton balls, a clean washcloth, cotton swabs, rubbing alcohol, diaper cream (optional) and a clean diaper and clothes. Make sure the room is nice and warm and choose a time when he is happy and not hungry (but not right after a feeding).

1 Hold LT on your knee or put him on a changing mat, strip him down to his undershirt and diaper, then wrap him up in a towel.

First Six Weeks

2 Dip a cotton ball in the water, squeeze out the excess and wipe around the eyes from the nose outward, using a separate ball for each eye to prevent cross-infection. Use a fresh ball for each ear, but don't clean inside because you don't want infection to get into the inner ear.

③ Dip the washcloth in the water, squeeze it out and gently wash the rest of his face and neck, including his creases. Now do his

hands. Dry him gently with the towel as you go.

④ LT's cord will shrivel and drop off in a week to ten days. Until his navel has healed, clean it with a cotton swab dipped in rubbing alcohol. After it has healed, you may use a cotton ball or washcloth on the area.

⑤ Remove the diaper and, if his diaper is dirty, clean him with wipes to remove the worst of it, then finish with baby soap (optional) and a wet washcloth. You should not pull back your baby boy's foreskin.

⑥ Dry him with a towel and let him relax without his diaper for a little while. If any other areas are dirty, wash them in the same way. You can then put diaper cream on the whole area, if you like, to prevent rashes. Don't feel like a failure if LT has a sore bottom; it happens to most babies at some point. If you're doing all the right things (as above) and changing him often, and he still gets a diaper rash, show it to your healthcare practitioner. It might be thrush, which will need treatment.

Bathtime

1. Fill the baby bath or a large plastic tub with a few inches of water, being careful to check the temperature. Have baby bath liquid or soap and shampoo on hand.

First Six Weeks

2 Follow the advice on washing his face and hands (page 92), then take off his undershirt and diaper.

3 Clean the diaper area, then wrap him in a towel and hold him firmly in the crook of your left arm (right, if you are left-handed), supporting his head and neck with your hand; you can then use your free hand to wash his hair with water and rinse it over the bath.

4 Unwrap him from the towel and put it under him, on your lap or the changing mat.

Soap him all over, avoiding his face. If you use baby bath liquid, you don't need additional soap.

5 Lower him into the bath, holding him firmly under one of his arms and supporting his head. Use your other hand to swoosh water over him.

6 Lift him out and onto a towel and pat him dry, paying careful attention to those creases under his arms and around his neck. This is the perfect time to give him a gentle massage with baby or almond oil.

7 Then put him to bed and get your partner to do the same for you (give you a massage, that is!).

8 When he's about 6 weeks and you feel confident handling him, try bathing with him—most babies love taking a bath with

their mom or dad, although you'll probably need another pair of hands available until he can sit up on his own. **Important:** Always check the temperature of the water before LT gets in.

First Six Weeks

DIAPERS

One thing is certain—LT is going to fill a lot of diapers. He won't care if they are cloth or disposable, he'll fill 'em up anyway. If you want to use cloth diapers, buy at least 24 because he will go through about

12 a day. Cloth diapers are cheaper than disposable, but not by much. After all, there's the added cost of plastic pants, disposable diaper liners, pins and laundering. However, some moms and dads just love

seeing rows of clean, white diapers blowing on the line in the sunshine.

Keeping things clean—cloth

Before washing cloth diapers, soak them in a bucket of diluted sterilizing fluid, following the manufacturer's instructions (after removing the diaper liner and contents, which can be flushed down the toilet).

Keeping things clean—disposable

Use the reseal tabs to wrap the disposable diaper, then wrap it up in a plastic bag.

Disposables are extremely convenient and are constantly improving for dryness. Once you've found

a good size and brand, buy in bulk. You will go through them quickly (probably 6 to 10 a day in the early weeks).

The cost is high, but they are self-contained—there is nothing else to buy.

Always wash your hands after changing diapers (whichever type) to keep those germs away. **Important:** Be extra careful

after LT has his polio shots
at 2, 4 and between 6 and
18 months—the live virus will be in his
stools for about a month.

Buy disposables
in bulk

Diapers

TAKING LT OUT

OK . . . so you've been home for a while, that's going great, and you've decided it's time for your first outdoor adventure. This might be a few days

after your baby's birth, or it could be a couple of weeks—whenever you feel ready.

Taking LT out is great. You get some exercise and a change of scenery, LT gets some fresh air, and lots of strangers go ga-ga over your baby. If you feel anxious

about getting everything ready, take your partner or a friend with you on the first few trips. Take it easy at first. Just go to the mall, or perhaps to a class or club for new parents where you can meet others who share your new interests (ask your health practitioner for recommendations or call your community center).

How will he travel?

Horizontal is best. If he's in a stroller, make sure he can lie flat. It's too soon to prop up his back. Slings are great. He usually stays snug and happy. The only problem might be loading and unloading, which isn't bad at first but can be awkward when he gets heavier.

In the car

If he's going in the car, the law requires a properly secured, backward-facing car seat. Put the car seat in the center of the back seat, never in the front. Make sure you have the appropriate seat for his size, and that it has a 3-point or 5-point harness.

Sunshine

LT's skin will burn easily, so in hot weather, protect him with sunscreen, a hat and light clothing. If taking him out in the stroller, use a canopy or umbrella.

How much should he wear?

As a general rule, dress LT more warmly than you are dressed—but don't think he has to be up to the hospital's sauna-like temperatures. Babies quickly lose heat from their heads, so in cold weather, he'll need a hat to keep in the warmth. Keeping him at a constant temperature is best. When taking him from a centrally heated house to the car, dress him warmly. If it's warm in the car, take off some layers so he doesn't overheat.

HEALTH AND SAFETY

Worrying about your new baby's well-being is completely natural. Everyone does it. Here are a few common worries and hazards, and tips on how to deal with them.

Worries and hazards—survival tips

🦀 **Fontanelles**—These are the two soft spots on LT's head. The back fontanelle closes at about 6 weeks. The front scalp bones don't join together until LT is 18 months old. These spots are tougher than you think because they are protected by a strong membrane. You can wash them when you wash LT's hair.

🎀 **Toddlers and animals**—Don't leave him alone at any time with either.

🎀 **Worried about his health or development?** See your healthcare practitioner—that's what she is there for.

🎒 **Colds, sickness, diarrhea**—Wash your hands after changing diapers. Sterilize all feeding equipment.

🎒 **SIDS (sudden infant death syndrome) or crib death**—Always put LT to sleep on his back. To avoid overheating, don't use too many blankets or too many layers of clothing. Place LT's feet at the end of the crib,

with covers up to his chest, so he can't wriggle down under them and become too hot. Don't smoke in any room your baby will be asleep or awake in.

🌸 **Safety**—Keep a smoke alarm and fire extinguisher in the house.

Scalds and burns—Put the affected area under the cold tap or in a bowl of cool water for 10 minutes, or until LT stops crying. Then wrap the area loosely in a clean, non-fluffy cloth, such as a cotton pillow case, or in a bandage, to avoid infection. Go to the hospital or call your healthcare practitioner.

✿ Choking—If he can cry, cough, or breathe, gently open his mouth, look inside and check for any object with your little finger. If you can't remove it or the baby can't cry, breathe or cough, call 911. Take a first-aid class to learn how to help a choking infant who cannot breathe. The American Red Cross or your healthcare practitioner can give you details.

Heat rash (tiny red spots mostly on the face)—Dress him in fewer layers of clothing—rash goes away without treatment.

Milia (common after first two weeks)—These look kind of nasty, but they usually go away without treatment. If not, seek medical advice.

🎀 **Stuffy nose (can't breathe easily when feeding or asleep)**—Try a couple of saline nose drops, then suction out the mucus. If LT can't sleep, place a cool-mist vaporizer in his room and place a pillow *under* the mattress (*not* on top, or he may suffocate) to elevate his head. Decongestants may also work, but always check with your pediatrician for a recommendation.

There are obviously many other potential hazards, but they are more likely to affect babies more than 6 weeks old. Take a baby first-aid course at your local community center or the American Red Cross. You'll be glad you did.

So that's about it

There are plenty of things you can do to get ready for your Little Terror's arrival, but, as you've probably already discovered, nothing can really prepare you for the experience, and you just have to take it one day at a time.

Like everything else in life, some people are naturals, while others have mixed feelings and have to work at it. The one sure thing is that every effort you make is rewarded somewhere along the line. Good or bad, it's important to share your feelings with your partner, or with a friend. To take care of LT, you need to take care of yourself and each other, Mom and Dad! If it seems rocky at first, remember that being a parent can be the most fulfilling experience of your life.

INDEX

First Six Weeks

NOTES:

NOTES: